P9-DNB-603

Pounds, Feet, and Inches

Holly Karapetkova

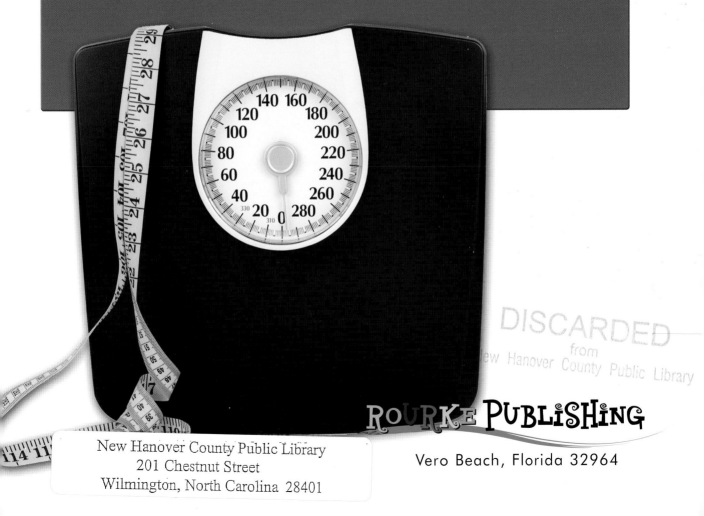

ROURKE PUBLISHING

Vero Beach, Florida 32964

www.rourkepublishing.com

PHOTO CREDITS: © Julia Nichols: Title Page; © Segheia Velusceac: 3; © JLBarranco: 5; © DGSpro: 7; © kledge: 7, 22; © Don Bayley: 9; © Kateryna Potrokhovo: 11; © Jaimie D. Travis: 11; © Skip ODonnell: 13, 23; © Stepan Popov: 15; © rusm: 17, 23; © blackred: 17; © janeff: 19; © DNY59: 19; © Stephan Coburn: 20; © Sandra G: 21

Editor: Meg Greve

Cover design by Nicola Stratford, bdpublishing.com

Interior Design by Heather Botto

Library of Congress Cataloging-in-Publication Data

Karapetkova, Holly.
  Pounds, feet, and, inches / Holly Karapetkova.
    p. cm. -- (Concepts)
  ISBN 978-1-60694-378-6 (hardcover)
  ISBN 978-1-60694-510-0 (softcover)
  ISBN 978-1-60694-568-1 (bilingual)
  1. Units of measurement--Juvenile literature. 2. Length measurement--Juvenile
literature. I. Title.
  QC90.6.K3686 2010
  530.8'1--dc22
                          2009015990

Printed in the USA

CG/CG

ROURKE PUBLISHING

www.rourkepublishing.com - rourke@rourkepublishing.com
Post Office Box 643328 Vero Beach, Florida 32964

What is a pound?

A pound measures weight.
It tells us how heavy
something is.

A loaf of bread is
about a pound.

What is a foot?

A foot measures length.
It can tell us how long,
how deep, or how tall.

A football is about a foot long.

Inches also measure length.
They are smaller than
a foot.

A paper clip is about an inch long.

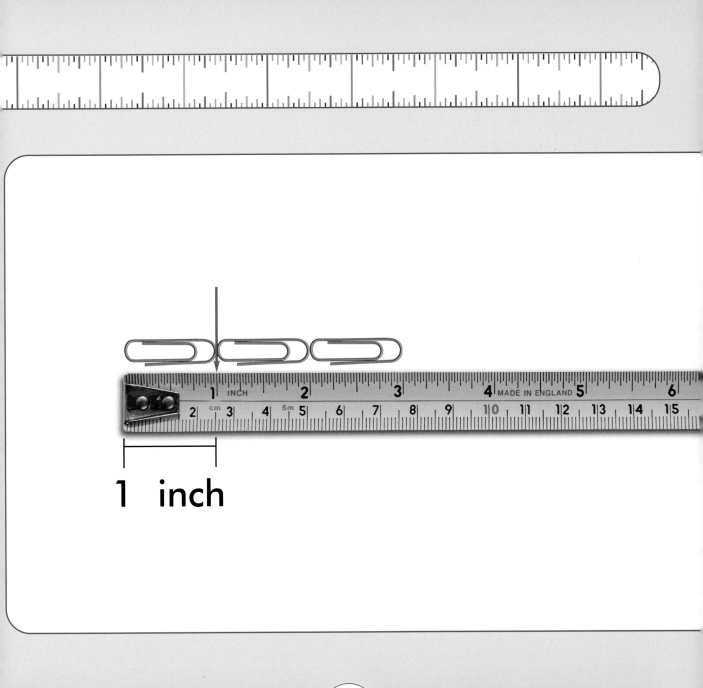

1 inch

How many inches are
in a foot?

TWELVE!

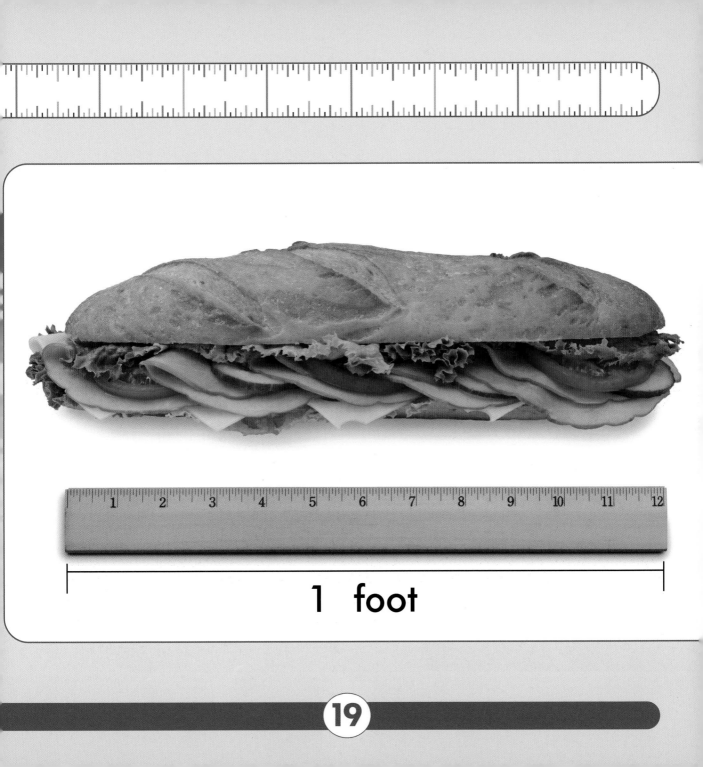

1 foot

How many pounds do YOU weigh?

How tall are YOU in feet and inches?

Converting Measurements from Customary to Metric

1 pound = 454 grams

(customary)   (metric)

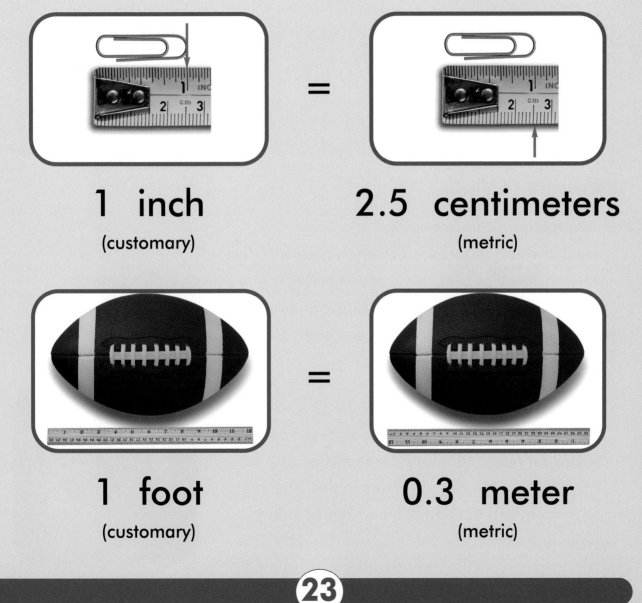

1 inch = 2.5 centimeters
(customary) (metric)

1 foot = 0.3 meter
(customary) (metric)

Index

Websites to Visit

www.funbrain.com/measure/
www.harcourtschool.com/activity/longer_shorter/
www.crickweb.co.uk/assets/resources/flash.php?&file=simplescales2
www.bbc.co.uk/schools/ks1bitesize/numeracy/measurements/
www.bbc.co.uk/schools/ks2bitesize/maths/activities/measures.shtml

About the Author

Holly Karapetkova, Ph.D., loves writing books and poems for kids and adults. She teaches at Marymount University and lives in the Washington, D.C., area with her son K.J. and her two dogs, Muffy and Attila.